Mary, Mother

Bob Chilcott

for SATB and piano or with organ and optional harp

vocal score

OXFORD
UNIVERSITY PRESS

OXFORD
UNIVERSITY PRESS

Great Clarendon Street, Oxford OX2 6DP,
United Kingdom

Oxford University Press is a department of the University of Oxford.
It furthers the University's objective of excellence in research, scholarship,
and education by publishing worldwide. Oxford is a registered trade mark of
Oxford University Press in the UK and in certain other countries

ISBN 978–0–19–356427–5

Music and text origination by Katie Johnston
Printed in Great Britain on acid-free paper by
Halstan & Co. Ltd, Amersham, Bucks.

Contents

Authors' note

Mary, Mother is a sequence of six carols that articulates the role of Mary in the Christmas story, very much from the human perspective. The author, Georgia Way, has written new, warm, and thoughtful texts that she introduces here:

These six carol texts came into being on the premise that Mary might be one of the best-known figures in the Christian world, but she might also be one of the least understood. Could the serene image of the Mother of God have become distant to us through her familiarity?

The challenge, then, was to find a way to make Mary's experiences, as a human woman, emotionally relevant to audiences today. This is perhaps why the sycamore tree became a central image. In the Bible, *Ficus sycomorus* is a way to see further, a way to see Jesus as he approaches. For me, this reflects one of the roles that music plays in our lives: a way to see further into emotional and spiritual truth.

If the sycamore casts a note of doubt, of instability, into Mary's emerging adulthood in the first of these six carols, then the remaining five work to resolve that instability. It is fitting to me that the sycamore should return in the final carol, a hymn to the regenerative power of the human spirit.

The carols that make up *Mary, Mother* can be performed individually or as a set. The accompaniment in this vocal score is designed to be played on the piano. The work was conceived with organ and harp accompaniment, and a full score and parts for this version are available for digital download.

Mary, Mother was written for St Martin's Voices and their Director, Andrew Earis, who gave the first performance at St Martin-in-the-Fields, London, on 18 December 2022.

Bob Chilcott and Georgia Way, June 2023

Duration: *c.*17 mins

For Andrew Earis and St Martin's Voices, St Martin-in-the-Fields, London;
commissioned with the generous support of an anonymous donor

Mary, Mother

1. A Child in Galilee

Georgia Way (b. 1992)

BOB CHILCOTT

Printed in Great Britain

OXFORD UNIVERSITY PRESS, MUSIC DEPARTMENT, GREAT CLARENDON STREET, OXFORD OX2 6DP

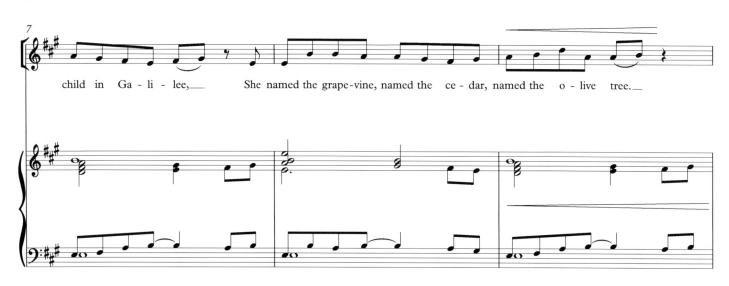

child in Ga - li - lee,___ She named the grape-vine, named the ce - dar, named the o - live tree.___

'Raise your voice, young Ma - ry,' called out the o - live tree,___ 'For

'Raise___ your voice,' called out the o - live tree,

'One

'Raise___ your voice,' called___ out the o - live tree,

one day I will crown you as Queen of Ga - li -

day I will crown you.'

- lee.'

A young girl, a girl in

When Ma - ry was a young girl, a girl in Ga - li - lee, She

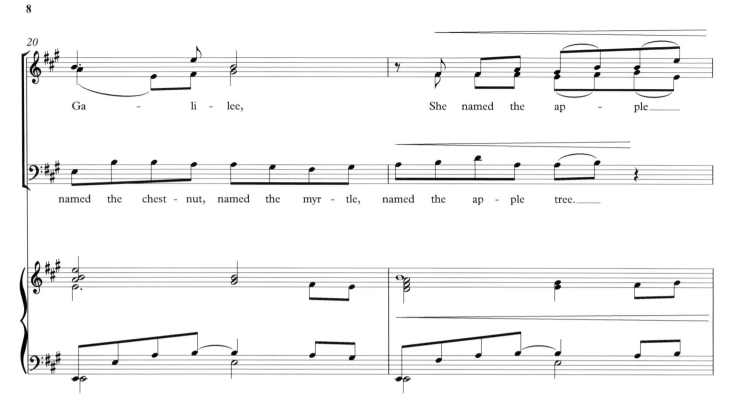

Ga - li - lee, She named the ap - ple ___

named the chest - nut, named the myr - tle, named the ap - ple tree.___

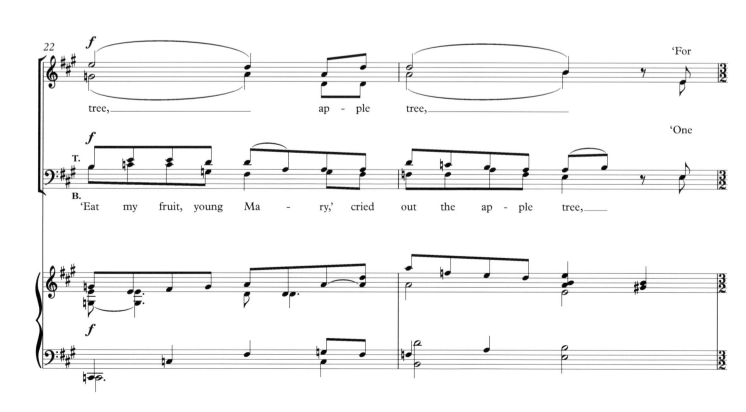

tree,___ ap - ple tree,___ 'For

'One

'Eat my fruit, young Ma - ry,' cried out the ap - ple tree,___

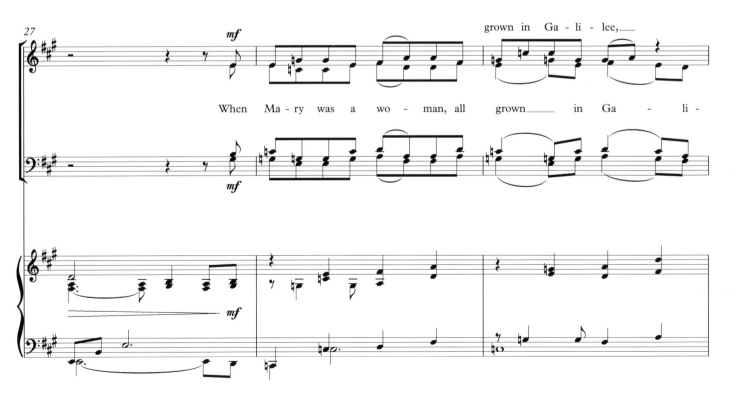

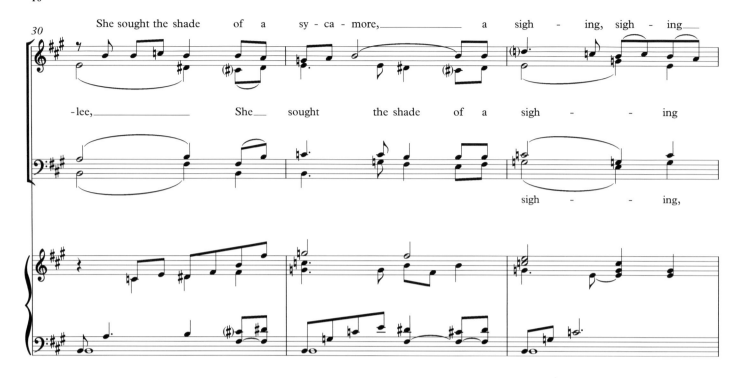

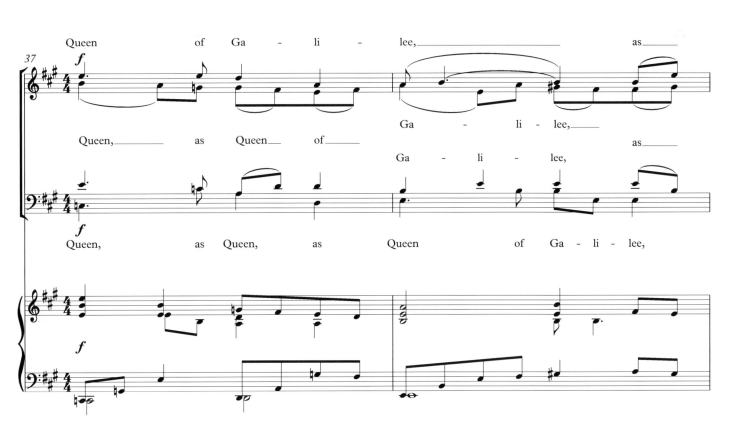

2. Carpentry Carol

sing, sy - ca - more, sing!_____ Sing, sy - ca - more, sing!_____

Build - ing a crib_____ for the fu - ture king._____

Build - ing a crib for the fu - ture king._____

She fell for his hands_ as gnarled as old roots, his

mind__ as young as green tim - ber._____ All__ the while__ he

he hummed__ to the tune: O sing, sy - ca - more, sing!___

hummed to the tune:_____

Me - lo - dies carved_____ for the heav'n - ly

Sing, sy - ca - more, sing!_____ Me - lo - dies carved for the heav'n - ly

feel - ing safe in a house on fire, and want - ing more.

and want - ing, want - ing more. O

sing, sy - ca - more, sing! Sing, sy - ca - more, sing!

man with the ten - der heart and hands,_____ carv - ing joy with a

plane and a lathe._____ O sing, sy - ca - more, sing!_____

Sing, sy - ca - more, sing!_____ Craft - ing the world for our heav'n - ly,

Craft - ing the world_____ for our heav'n - ly,

3. *After the angel*

And aft - er the an - gel, Ma - ry dreamt.

Lord, she prayed, you have locked the gate, locked is the gate to the com - mon pas - ture,

22

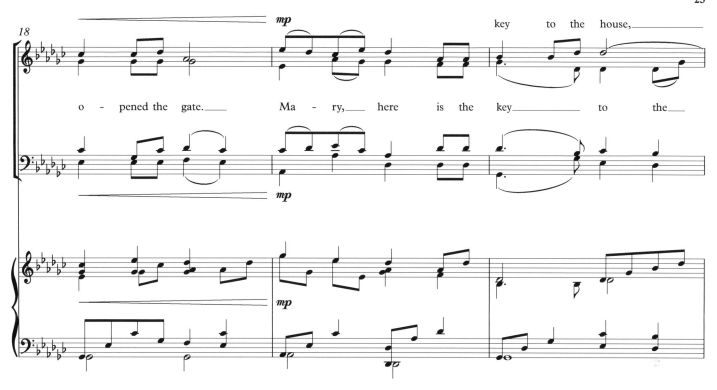

key to the house,

o - pened the gate. Ma - ry, here is the key to the

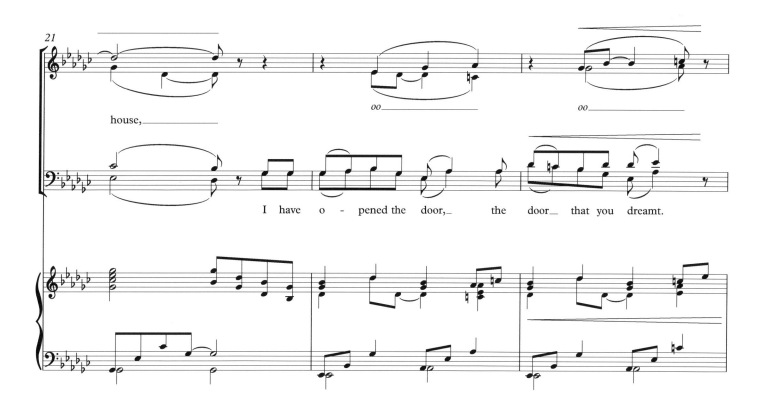

house,

oo   oo

I have o - pened the door, the door that you dreamt.

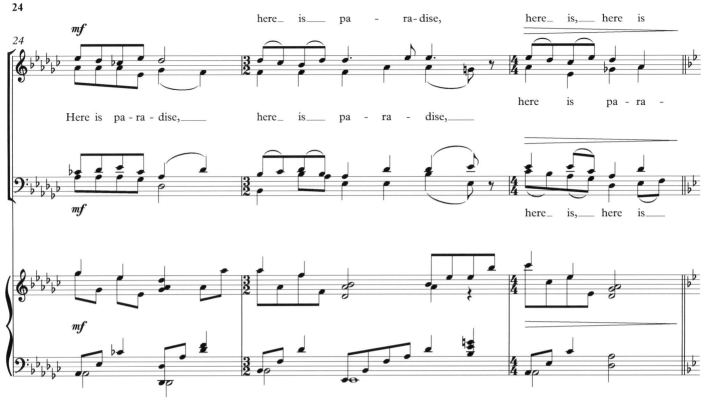

4. Walking Carol

Eight for wish-ing___ we could all go home.

road,___ end-less road.

Nine for the months of growth and pain, Ten for the cen-sus and tax-es to pay, E -

-le-ven for Jo - seph, wor-ried and tired, And twelve for the joy of the un-born child,___

5. Dear heart

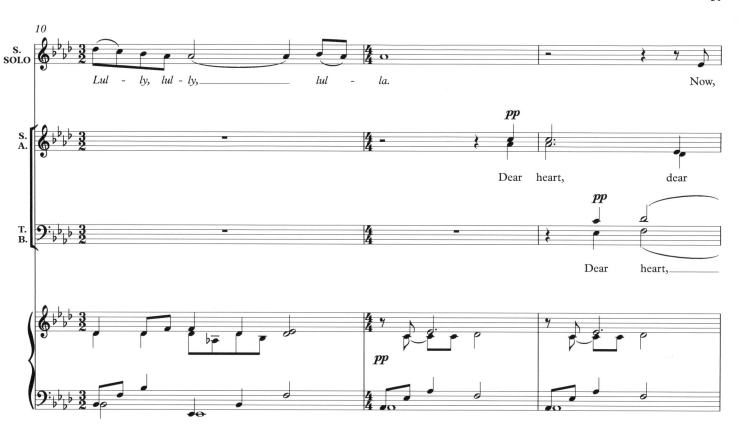

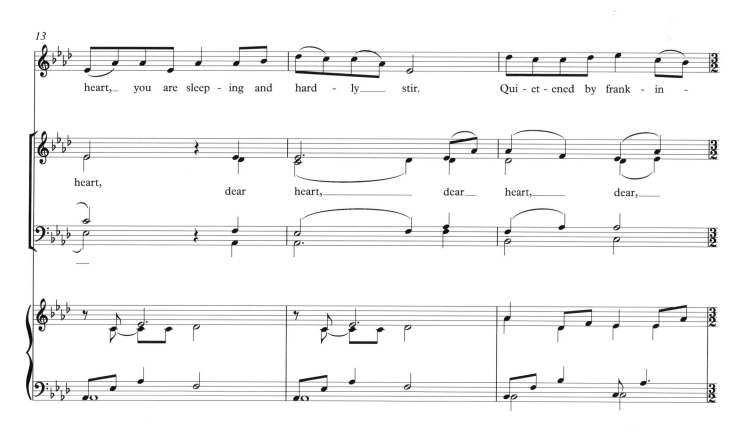

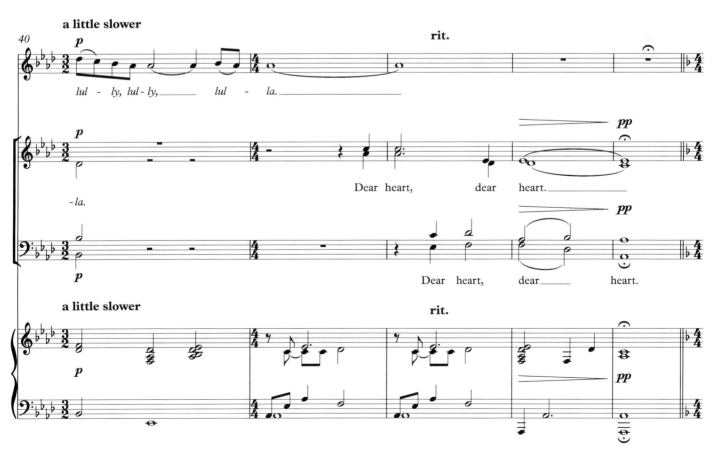

6. Hymn

-lu - ia!__ In ex - cel - sis__ glo - ri - a!

SOPRANO DESCANT

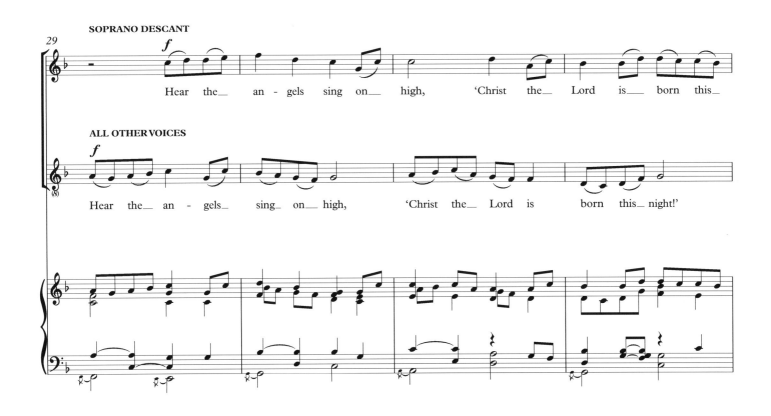

Hear the__ an - gels sing on__ high, 'Christ the__ Lord is__ born this__

ALL OTHER VOICES

Hear the__ an - gels__ sing__ on__ high, 'Christ the__ Lord is__ born this__ night!'